teresa wilms montt

SENTIMENTAL DOUBTS

translated and with an introduction by
jessica sequeira

THIS IS A SNUGGLY BOOK

Translation and Afterword Copyright © 2020
by Jessica Sequeira.
All rights reserved.

ISBN: 978-1-64525-024-1

SENTIMENTAL DOUBTS

TERESA WILMS MONTT was born on September 8, 1893 in Viña del Mar, Chile, into an elite, well-connected family. Her first book, *Inquietudes sentimentales*, consisted of fifty poems with surrealist features, while her second, *Los tres cantos*, explored eroticism and spirituality. Both books enjoyed great success in Argentine intellectual circles. In 1918, she moved to Madrid, where she published two works widely recognized by Spanish literary critics: *En la quietud del mármol* and *Anuarí*. Upon returning to Buenos Aires in 1919, she published her fifth book, *Cuentos para hombres que todavía son niños*. She died in 1921, in Paris, from an overdose of Veronal.

JESSICA SEQUEIRA was born in San Jose, California in 1989, and currently lives in Santiago de Chile. Her works include the novel *A Furious Oyster* (Dostoyevsky Wannabe), and the collection of essays *Other Paradises: Poetic Approaches to Thinking in a Technological Age* (Zero). Her translations include Adolfo Couve's *When I Think of My Missing Head* (Snuggly) and Liliana Colanzi's *Our Dead World* (Dalkey Archive).

CONTENTS

Introduction / 7

Sentimental Doubts / 19

INTRODUCTION

"Inquietude" is no longer a word much used, even less so in the plural. Its mixture of restlessness and disturbance, both physical and mental, is the theme of the prose poems in *Inquietudes sentimentales* by Teresa Wilms Montt, first published in 1917 in Buenos Aires, after she'd left an entire life behind her in Santiago: her husband, her parents, the convent where she'd been confined for supposedly committing adultery, and her two daughters, whom she was forbidden from seeing. "Inquietude" is not the same as agitation, for during the moment of action itself, one has no time to think, let alone sink into the darkest reaches of the soul. Inquietude is the racing heart, the muttering mind, the explosion of doubts that only truly emerge when one is, at last, in a place of calm.

How to ferry these tricky emotions of the original text into the present? When words grow dated, they lose their luminousness, their vibrancy, and become objects. They can sound dated. The word "inquietudes" is rare now, in plural or in singular, and to render it literally would suggest a preciousness that the raw original text does not have. Language reflects shifts in the priority that society gives to emotions; a similar decay in resonance has affected the word "hysteria".

After running through the options of concerns (too legalistic), anxieties (unpoetic) or restlessnesses (but this isn't really a plural noun in English), I settled on "doubts", which, in its instability, seems to best capture Wilms Montt's tone. Throughout her poems, doubt and its accompanying emotional and physical restlessness are clear topics, so much so that Hamlet is even explicitly referenced—a somewhat surprising allusion, and a reminder of the education that Wilms Montt received.

Shakespeare is slightly misquoted, it's true, although in this shifting world of references it isn't clear if this is intentional. Wilms Montt frequented artistic circles in Buenos Aires with Jorge Luis Borges and Victoria Ocampo, among others, writers who delighted in intellectual play and had no problem coyly adapting a quote for poetic purposes, if they thought it necessary—or simply interesting—to do so. Wilms Montt became personally friendly with several figures in this environment, and it's unclear how much the closeness extended to literary influence.

The original edition of *Sentimental Doubts* features black-and-white drawings by Gregorio López Naguil, which provide a sinuous, mysterious atmosphere in rich dialogue with the Eastern themes of Wilms Montt's text. López Naguil also provided illustrations for the Argentine writer Carlos Muzzio Sáenz-Peña, the author of several books including a translation of Omar Khayyam's *Rubáiyát* (1916), *Las veladas de Ramadán: Cuentos, apólogos y leyendas de la Persia islamita* [Evenings of Ramadan: Stories, Apologues and Legends of Islamic Persia] (1916), *El babú de Narayana* [The Babu of Narayana] (1918) and *Samsara: poemas cortos* [Samsara: Short Poems] (1919). These among others in the Argentine milieu—again, including Borges—were intrigued by Eastern legends, myths and aesthetics.

Many texts taking up Eastern philosophy were being published in Buenos Aires at the time, ranging from Joaquín V. González's translation of Kabir's poems, based on a translation into English by Rabindranath Tagore, to Ricardo Güiraldes' mystical poetry inspired by his travels in India, to dozens of works on theosophy and occult sciences. Two major literary figures from Spain with whom Wilms Montt is connected, and who praised and promoted her work during her lifetime—Ramón del Valle Inclán and Juan Ramón Jiménez (who called her work a "mysticism of love and pain")—were also deeply engaged with Eastern culture.

This atmosphere of intellectual curiosity about alternative traditions may well have had its effect on Wilms Montt, in search of new sources of inspiration beyond those of the Catholic church which had served both as a consolation and as a source of resentment in Chile. Could Wilms Montt's devotional poetry addressed to an ethereal Anuarí, who may or may not always correspond to a human body, be read alongside the mystical bhakti poets of India, where the erotic poem to the lover and the divine form the dual reality that resolves into oneness?

Besides these currents, an influx of European ideas was entering the country at this time, in part due to the flood of immigrants to Argentina in the first two decades of the twentieth century, in part due to a taste in the literary élite for whatever came from abroad. Paris was considered to be the center of the literary world, and Victoria Ocampo's cosmopolitan *Sur* brought ideas from France, as well as other countries, to a Buenos Aires that prided itself on prosperity and civilization, even as it grappled with its new urban population and the new ideas of anarchism and socialism that immigrants brought with them.

A list of short books published as part of the *La Novela Semanal* series, founded in 1917 to encourage the popular *nouvelle* and eventually publishing many of the country's best-known writers, bears witness in its titles to an interest in literary currents abroad, with books taking up French decadent style, Eastern themes and new trends in psychology and medicine. Wilms Montt's work can be framed in this social context, as well as in the emotional context she chose to present.

Sentimental Doubts explores lovesickness in precisely these terms, as a sickness. Pain, poverty, illness and madness are all romanticized as truer ways of understanding the world and reaching its essence. As Wilms Montt herself says at one point, she doesn't feel that she can make art except by being sad, and by identifying with a beggar. The reader is left with these troubling assertions. There is indeed a strong element of *abajismo* in the work, the degradation of the self and identification with what is lower, to achieve a greater intensity of living. Twilight, decay and shadow run throughout as flickering in-between spaces, working to unsettle and stir up anguish.

Subtle references to French literature abound, especially to Baudelaire's tone and phrases, such as with the *campana cascada* which seems a reference to his *cloche fêlée*, and in the use of French loanwords such as *chut* for "hush" and *vitreaux* to refer to stained-glass windows. The grotesque images of the mad bacchante, Pierrot, the faun, the evil fairy and the piano are likely also borrowed. But the influences of Wilms Montt go further than this. Life is described as a carnival of illusion, a fundamental Eastern idea that Wilms Montt here adopts. Other Eastern references are present, as for instance with the mention of the terrifying Chinese masks on the wall, inexplicably laughing in the face of her suffering.

Throughout the whole book, a kind of mysticism is apparent. Love is defined as a lack of substance, the opposite of physical objects.

Nothingness is a fascination. Wilms Montt wants to surrender, yet not entirely, as she makes clear with her bathetic imagery of the soul as a gladiator. She identifies with Nature, yet describes the way that Nature turns against her, cruel and unfeeling. The narcotics to which she was already privately addicted during this period, along with the ether she enjoyed in social company, perhaps contributed something to this mood as well.

The same year that *Sentimental Doubts* was published, a young man named Horacio Ramos Mejía killed himself in front of her, an occurrence that formed the subject matter for Wilms Montt's next two books *Anuarí* and *In the Stillness of Marble*. Mysteries linger, however, and it would be a mistake to read Wilms Montt's work only through this tragedy. One asks where the name comes from, and whether there was a single Anuarí or multiple, an invocation given to diverse lovers.

In *Sentimental Doubts*, the Anuarí is still described as a living, breathing, vital presence, and the event of his death does not form the center of the work, as it does in the two books that follow. Yet Death is already present as backdrop or premonition, and *Sentimental Doubts* (Buenos Aires, 1917), *Anuarí* (Madrid, 1918) and *In the*

Stillness of Marble (Madrid, 1918) can be read as a sort of trilogy in their similar subject matter, each with a slightly different style.

In this first work, a sort of prologue to the other two, Wilms Montt's prose poetry is thicker and less direct, with many anecdotes remaining oblique and not fully understood. Wilms Montt had already left the convent when she wrote this, parting from her children, a separation that must have affected her painfully. Yet in *Sentimental Doubts* it is not entirely clear to which particular episodes the scenes with her pain and sick child refer, or the nature of her current relationship to Anuarí. Specific moments of what we might now call trauma have been blurred and transfigured beyond recognition.

How much comes from Wilms Montt's life and how much has been fictionalized to sharpen descriptions with imaginative fancy, on behalf of the construction of a more intense emotional record? Certain references do not necessarily find context in a close reading of her diary, a similarly stylized document. The "creatures" addressed throughout are likely her daughters, but the allusions are indirect, and other different sorrows (Anuarí, her angst at witnessing poverty, her own self-doubts) seem to be layered over one another as separate glazes with interpenetrating tints, baked to the hard vibrant finish of a color that's entirely new.

The famous Chilean literary critic "Alone", a contemporary of Wilms Montt, had the following to say about our poet: "Did she have a spark of genius? Or, with the negligence of a pretty woman, did she stir about phrases as empty as fake pearls? The pages of her works constantly produce this double impression of an astonishment that makes one suspicious. Just as she could never completely surrender to Nature, her reader resists and admires and sympathizes with her, while also doubting [. . .] In the midst of a dizzying lyricism, jumping from one image to another infinitely far away, Teresa Wilms Montt shows touches of an unexpected and natural ingenuousness that charms."

Rather than read these poems autobiographically, it seems more fulfilling to approach them as a shifting play of doubts and questions, as the title itself suggests. This is a work of the fantastical imagination with a certain romanticization of sickness and madness, distilled into images such as the Pierrot. Yet Wilms Montt is open to many influences, and she writes several poems that take everyday objects (even, at one point, the mailbox) as her point of departure. There is wretched pain and great loneliness, and an emphasis on the idea of the transitory nature of our lives; yet not all is bleak. As the writing of Wilms Montt makes clear, there is also great beauty to be found in restlessness, impressionistic shifting, the temporary glimmers of light on water.

"Doubts", as a word and concept, also has a religious charge, of course, of which Wilms Montt is well aware. She subverts it, along with "thirst" and "resurrection", as a part of her general literary technique of turning pain into eroticism, sadness into seduction, doubt into assertion. From her first lines, she claims that she is not writing literature, and this is her opening move to implant in the reader inquietudes which correspond to those felt by herself.

—Jessica Sequeira

SENTIMENTAL DOUBTS

PREFACE

In offering these pages to the reader, I have not attempted to write literature. My intention has been only to give a release to my spirit, as one gives a release to a torrent contained for a long time, which floods the area around it with its spreading.

I write as I would laugh or cry, and these lines enshrine all the spontaneity and sincerity of my soul.

There they go, without asking for kindness or commentary: there they go with the same naturalness that the bird flies, the stream tumbles, the plant germinates . . .

I

The light of the lamp, weakened by a violet screen, faints on the table.

The objects take on the sleepwalking tint of a sickly dream; one might say that a consumptive hand has caressed the atmosphere, leaving behind an aristocratic languidness.

An impious bell repeats the hour and makes me understand that I live, and also reminds me that I suffer.

I suffer from a strange evil that poisons me like narcotics: lovesickness, misunderstood greatness, infinite ideals.

A disease urges me to live within another heart, to rest from the bitter task of feeling when I live within myself.

As the thirsty long for water, so do I yearn to hear a voice promising me enchanting sweetnesses; I yearn for a child's little hand to rest on my eyelids tired of keeping vigil, to calm my rebellious, adventurous spirit.

Thus do I desire to die, like the lamplight as it falls over objects, dissolving into gentle flickering shadows.

II

I walked along the sleepy road one dusky evening.

The autumn trees raised their stripped arms to the wind in who knows what tragic gesture of supplication; and the mountains, red with fury under the setting sun, threatened to collapse into the gentle river like an ill woman.

Nature!

Soul that I feel within me and isn't mine. I understand you in your enormous, secret greatness.

Just as I penetrate into the beauty of the heavenly king, so do I observe the sentimental tragedy of the little blade of grass, which wants to be a tree and struggles against animals' hooves, carts' wheels and man's indifference, and dies at last, crushed against a donkey's nose.

Nature, if you are so kind to the one born great, why are you not also so to the one born wretched?

You cannot hide anything from me, Nature; for I am in you, as you are in me: fused to each other like metals into a single piece.

You are mine, Nature, with all of the treasures concealed in you.

Mine, is the gold that gleams, fascinating the gnomes in the depth of the pits; mine, the silver that plots with you, preparing macabre plans to make men destroy each other; mine, is the diamond, majestic in its simplicity; mine, your lava blood that flows boiling through volcanoes; mine, are your flowers and your divine lakes; mine, your mountains and valleys; Nature, you are mine, for my feet have put out roots that pierce through the globe, and I have drawn sap from you.

Mine, are your misfortunes too; mine, your infinite pains of a mother; mine are the cradle of Insult and the refuge of Death . . .

Nourished by your sap, I grew until I felt my head hold itself high and look toward the infinite, as toward the younger brother of thought.

III

A very sweet-smelling carnation dies bleeding.

It's a heart split open on a Sèvres plate.

Strange feelings are produced in me by its scattered petals; I should say, prostituted lips, fresh wounds from a dagger.

I have nothing, I want nothing; my aching head, ill from a strange disease, surrenders itself on the table, heavy as a marble slab.

IV

Creatures: if pain were not as boundless as the infinite, I would have burst its limits.

Because beyond everything that the mind can imagine is my inconsolable soul, enclosed in its silence of grief.

Creatures: I call to you, not with the voice God has given those men who love speech, but with another voice, created in the depths of my being by the immense desolation of sorrow.

I live from memories of you, creatures; my heart is covered with tears, tears that make my acts of kindness fertile, as rain gives flowers to earth.

Creatures: your names are the key to a sacred tabernacle, before which I offer up my soul in sacrifice; they are the blessed secret of my life, which has never turned to desecration.

If God exists, if his justice and his grandeur are not a farce, then on the day of my death, redeemed by the immense pain of having lost you, he will let me bear on my lips the very tender impression of your chaste kisses; and on my brow, the freshness of your adored little hands.

V

A gust of icy wind put out the lamp; the doors shuddered, the curtains bulged and through the sky, a flash of lightning streaked by with the rumble of a torrent.

With delight I await the sister of my spirit, come now to devastate the earth.

Tempest! I'll expose my uncovered head to the fury of your lightning, and surrender myself, amazed, to the rhythm of your thunderbolts.

Tempest! In your fury, I want to suffocate this arrogance of mine.

VI

Mirror! Why do you reflect me as young? Why the grotesque joke? You see how the ills of old age and the signs of fatigue parade past my eyes; you see how my tormented soul aspires only to dreaming sleep.

Mirror, you are my twin brother and know my life better than God.

You know what clear purities lulled me in youth; you know the enthusiasm of a bird I had for all beautiful things; you know my tragic devotion to the legends of enchanted princes . . . You know that melodious music and gentle songs made me weep, and that a word of affection made me the slave to another soul, and you know, too, that everything I dreamed had a heartbreaking reality.

I've emerged wounded from the bitter trial, bleeding, for I have left behind pieces of my being.

You, ironic mirror, know my life is nothing but one long agony, with a strange procession of carnivalesque laughter.

Remember that the ringing of handbells does not only announce holidays; behind it often also comes the cart of lepers.

VII

Two breasts of a disturbing whiteness, two eyes drunk with tears and a bold sensual hand crossed my path. An indefinable voice, like the gasp of hysterical sob, said to me: "I am eroticism, come!"

And I went; I went, following that outlandish bacchante, as the steel blade follows the magnet.

I went, drawn by mystery . . . My lips froze, and in my throat there was a clamp of iron.

My gaze grew damp, my eyes were as pale as diamonds in alcohol . . .

I came back, and my lips were withered, and my eyes could not see, and my hands were bitter against themselves, wishing only to destroy one other.

And in my soul, like a mark of fire, I bore the most horrible deception.

It was not there; that mad bacchante did not bring a cure for my lovesickness.

VIII

You, garden, do not have a soul. I've walked pale with suffering through your flowers, and they held not a tear for me.

They kept themselves upright, full of sun, flirting with air; and the palm trees, in their solemn poses, kept waving like languid arms in moments of love.

The grass, where my despairs tumbled, did not lose its velvet calm.

You, garden, do not have a soul. You've seen me faint from pain and your birds kept singing with the most joyful chirping, bringing together their little beaks in the intoxication of passion.

You, garden, do not have a soul . . .

IX

The gods sheathed in their Olympian tunics have come for a visit. All retain their majesty except Love, who entertains herself twirling pirouettes under lamplight, and with her arrows threatens a papier-mâché Japanese woman whose shape marks a dark stain on the bed.

    The pulsing of shadows is as gentle as the fluttering of a dream butterfly on a flower.

X

In the city of the dead there was a stillness of marble.

The statues of the tombs maintained a sepulchral calm, receiving on their backs the brilliance of stars like drops of light.

Nothing disturbed the silence.

On the stump of a cypress, the black bird of fateful omens, head under its wing, awaited the message of the dead to the living. My slow steps echoed in the sad avenues like muffled blasphemies; but my hands, closely joined in the form of prayer, seemed to rise from the earth like two bound doves.

I walked, and at each gloomy tomb my spirit stopped, making out some sign of life, a lament, a sob . . .

The desolate icy calm persisted in the enclosure of those asleep for eternity, their hearts consumed by earth.

It began to grow light, and only the bright star of dawn remained in the sky, a devout altar candle.

My ecstatic soul, filled with belief, waited for the voice of the sublime Maestro to tear through the silence and say: "Lazarus, rise up and go."

XI

The walls drip red ink which trickles to the carpet, forming a scarlet pool.

Strange figures with narrow eyes hand me a rare flower with a single petal; these eyes like painted beads, slanting with defiant cynicism, fascinate me, and sweep me into the esoteric world of morbid imagination.

To avoid delirium, I have drawn back the curtains, and the shadows conspiring against me have slipped through the openings, sly as quicksilver.

The sun says goodbye to my windows, emptying its dying reflections onto the glass and tinting my balcony yellow.

XII

Her little hands were like two restless butterflies, two buds just opened to the breeze.

Her little mouth was a pitcher of rubies, which by nature's whim had acquired life and were bleeding.

Her eyes were two lakes under the serenity of a full moon, where all the blue of ether was hidden.

And her face was a sheet of marble, on which destiny had written rare unfathomable figures in lapis lazuli.

Her hair was dissolved topaz, which scattered in my arms, flashing like the diamond-threads of stars.

How lovely she was!

How lovely and how tender!

She came to the world to make me feel the meaning of adoration, to teach my lap the sweetest of burdens and to awaken in my heart the holiest and most beautiful of ideals.

And she left . . . !

She left that reality of a dream.

Is it possible, my God, to say the dead are lonelier than I am?

XIII

As the waves of the sea build up with the blowing of wind, so the intensity of my pain builds when, head sunk between my arms, I start to remember.

I'm even jealous of those beings who have no bread, but possess what all the riches in the world cannot give me.

Someone who loves them, who listens with tenderness to their complaints about life and shares their amazement in rare moments of happiness.

In the solitude of my boudoir, I never find the proof that my existence is pleasing to another being; nothing says to me: "You may rest, because you live in another heart."

If I cry, my tears freeze. They already know that no one will come to wipe them away. If I despair, I must find consolation alone, imposing a tyrannical will over myself.

And that's how I live: always restless, always alone, deceiving myself with illusions that I do not really possess, as children do when they play with their hobby horse, truly believing in it.

What does it matter to the world to see a sleepwalker who feels pain? It doesn't touch their hearts. They entertain themselves, looking as if at a curiosity.

Only those beings who suffer have a soul; only they can understand the sobbing of another being and, with deep compassion, clasp the hand bereft of caresses.

The nights repeat so often when, head sunk between my arms, I start to remember . . .

XIV

You appeared, Anuarí, when with eyes blind and arms outstretched, I was looking for you.

You appeared, and there was a burst of life in my soul; all of my inner flowers opened, and the bird of festive days sang.

And now you are mine, like the water that slips between my fingers, like the shadows that as they flee, grow longer with day; you are mine, with the doubt that I am always losing you.

I love your eyes, which make me fall at your feet as evening languishes. I love them because they pierce through my pupils, as light does through windows, taking pleasure in the contemplation of my soul.

In them I've seen the key to my secret yearning, the source of my spiritual delirium.

Anuarí, the embers of your gaze have consecrated me as a woman.

In the stillness of night and with hands joined, I've surrendered my soul to you.

XV

I wished to love, and in a supreme effort, to cross through infinite spaces.

To love and die of love!

To suffer and bend over until I touched the earth, like the broken branch of a tree.

I wished to live, and in my yearning possess everything . . . I wished to die.

XVI

A morose gladiator measures out the paving stones of the ground with an exaggerated step.
    Over his rigid body, invisible arrows collide.
    The noise they make when they break on the pavement is the peal of a cracked bell.
    This grotesque gladiator is my uneasy spirit.

XVII

"To die, to sleep, perchance to dream..."

Wretched are the beings who, like Hamlet, bear tragic doubt in the spirit.

To die while sleeping...

To sleep when dead...

To dream, without realizing that life is gone...

XVIII

Silence has strangled the night, and I'm living the true life.

Hush! The scornful one, wrapped in her intangible cloak, moves through the spaces cautiously, with her cautious step of a maleficent cat.

There you go by, thief of souls, traitorous Death; I challenge you . . . Come and steal my love who is sleeping, in surrender to me.

We'd clash in titanic struggle; he's stronger than you and would defeat you.

You'll continue to move through infinite spaces, but with the bitter deception of knowing that there is something you must respect, despite your absolute imperial power.

Anuarí, while you were sleeping and your body had the stillness of a statue, I drank up the soul you trustingly left to me.

I sipped you through my lips, as a bee does the essence of a flower.

Anuarí, with your beauty, with the light that radiates with goodness from your entire gaze, you alone soothe my illness.

XIX

On the corner of my street, there is a mailbox who never enjoys a day of rest. Every time I lean my head out the window, my eyes stumble across him and send him a friendly, compassionate gaze.

Poor mailbox! How ridiculous he seems with his head eternally in the air, receiving the lashings and the rawness of the four seasons! His toothless mouth is always open, waiting for those papers they call letters to be slipped in, carrying all of their human passions and turmoil.

How much bitterness there must be in the heart of a mailbox; how much bitterness, and how much experience!

But this poor rigid mailbox cannot say a thing. Whoever created him took good care to leave him mute.

And there he is, fixed at the corner, impassive, preserving his servile appearance, always red in sun or rain.

Mailbox: I understand your wise resigned soul, your poor soul imprisoned in an ugly metal block.

When you feel sad, and feel that those eyes you don't have are growing damp, think of your brothers, the balconies and street lamps, and your sisters, the chimneys and weather vanes, which like you are enslaved and receive no caresses but the wind's, sharp at times, but all the same caresses.

Mailbox, you have my sympathy and that of every being who, like me, has found a soul in you.

Every afternoon, after the sun sets, I'll come to you and slide in a letter that speaks of many tender things, to relieve the burden of your life.

Take care the postman does not steal your secret. Watch out, mailbox, for men are very bad and will laugh at the purest love.

XX

It's raining . . .

Drops of water sing inside the zinc pipes.

The light from the lamps has become more intimate; the pictures look around with a confidential air, and the purr of the cat has the gentleness of a violin with muffler.

My heart is waiting. I've deceived it by making it believe that tonight a beloved one will come.

Poor heart with its illusion of hope! Isn't life an eternal looking forward to something which never arrives? . . .

It's raining . . .

In my boudoir are the perfume of withered flowers, remembered scents, the sadness of past loves.

My heart is waiting . . .

It's raining . . .

XXI

At the twilight hour, I've come to look at myself in the pond, and it has returned my image from the depths with the inscrutable stillness of mystery.

So must the image of a woman be reflected in the pupils of her dead beloved.

I'd like to understand nothing, to be born again; for the diverse lives of the world to penetrate into my spirit, little by little, taking pleasure in presenting me with marvelous surprises.

Twilight has the beauty of the fleeting which passes, carrying away shreds of the soul: pure idealisms, cut-short thoughts like unfinished works of art.

All of us carry a twilight and a daybreak in our spirits. My spirit tends more to death than to life; it aspires more to sleep than to wakefulness; it leans toward the earth where it will find its bed.

XXII

A black shadow passed my door, eyes closed and a finger on her lips.

She disappeared around the corner of the hallway.

When I returned to my boudoir, I saw that the pearls of my necklace had died, and that the mirrors were blurred . . .

XXIII

Nothing moves in the boudoir.

He's sleeping.

My soul and the soul of things are suspended, keeping watch over his rest.

On the warm bed, mingling with the satin of the duvet, his transparent body is stretched out.

His eyes are two petals of a gigantic violet, and his hair, on the whiteness of the pillow, imitates a blue velvet heart.

Love, glory, happiness . . . !

You come smash yourselves on this unmoving figure like light against a prism, and humbly submerge yourself in the magnificent glow of different colors, to adorn his image with the vestments of a god.

Anuarí, beautiful spirit of goodness. Everything remains unmoving: time has withheld its gasp so as not to awaken dream, which has slept here in my boudoir; and I, ecstatic, have clutched my wounded heart, my heart sick from a strange illness.

XXIV

The wind swirls the dry leaves on the sidewalk corners.

The little old man of the neighborhood dressed in ignoble rags, an ironic costume of poverty, hunchbacked under the weight of a sack that treats his weak shoulders badly, looks with greed at the bags in a rubbish bin, left forgotten by the door of a house.

At this moment the old man's entire aim is to get hold of the disgusting filth contained in the bin. And this being has two feet and goes about with head held high, like those who have a soul.

Wicked destroyer, poverty, you drag away more beings than death!

How many men there are who, lacking even a pallet to sleep on, go rest under the bridges of the river and take mud for a coat!

What sarcasm! And above, in the sky, a white sheet covers those winged spirits who have not suffered, and do not know the horrible key that shuts away the word "live".

And these men who are happy, since cruel luck has spoiled them, set out in their vessel of indifference, bursting with life and rowing through a sea of blood, the blood of their fellow men.

I am not happy, nor could I ever be, because then I would not be a sister to the wretched; because then I would not have the boundless soul of indulgence.

XXV

In the cradle of my arms, still warm with the life of Her, "the little one", the icy shape of separation now shelters.

The ardent groove her little head left on my shoulder serves as a well for my tears, which flow with inexhaustible anguish.

And those little shoes, such a tender relic, which retain the blossomlike shape of her feet, are the casket of my kisses, and they, ay!, have no soul to return my caresses.

The dresses of hers I keep with me are pious, because when I lay them on the bed, they help me to evoke her adored little body.

And her lock of hair, which like a ray of forgotten sun I wear hanging as a prisoner around my neck, gives me a sensation of her ermine warmth.

How many nights the dawn has taken me by surprise, tightly clutching in my arms these remainders of lost happiness!

Creature! . . . Creatures! In what horrible desolation have I been left; in what cold of a mountain plateau does my heart live?

XXVI

Through the streets of dawn goes Pierrot, driven mad.

The immaculate white costume that sheathed the legend is now a dirty bloodstained rag.

His fantastic sleeves, which had the appearance of wings when he invoked the moon, now continue their shaky movement as two tatters, snagging on the stones and thorns of the road.

Pierrot has lost his ideal; Pierrot knows his love is not in the moon, and so he wanders, eyes devastated, holding back the howl of pain inside his chest.

Those poor lips, which once drank delight from other lips of rose, now display the enigmatic form of a poisoned ulcer.

Pierrot, without being conscious of it, has reached the countryside; his exhausted feet cannot follow him, and he falls like clothes without a body, at the edge of a puddle where the moon laughs.

XXVII

One . . . two . . . three! Now the hour has died in the arms of Time.

There was a shudder in the bell tower, and the scream of a siren tore through the silence.

Anuarí, my benevolent spirit, from the pavilion where he has been laid, lowers his gaze toward me.

The tranquil bliss of dream fills my soul.

If only dying were like this, so gentle!

Anuarí, give me your pure intentions; give me the balsam caresses of your intangible beauty and the exquisiteness of your magician's spirit; give me the kiss of your mouth, made material in a vast range of tendernesses.

Anuarí, my best song and the purest of my praises will be for you; there will never be a shadow in my heart, if you stay within it.

Another hour that dies has made the night weep. For me neither time nor death exist, when I am beneath the love in your eyes, Anuarí.

XXVIII

I penetrated with fervor into the abandoned temple.

The dream of Time had put its cadaverous rigidity into the walls and pointed arches.

The altars flaunted their embroideries of old greenish-gold, and their dull bronzes covered in gray dust had the ominous impression of having forgotten life.

The statues of the saints had fallen asleep from ecstasy, wrapped in the folds of their faux marble tunics; and the fingers of their marble hands continued to point at the place where their sacred chimeras disappeared.

The organ was mute, it had been mute for a century; and the mother-of-pearl of its keys piously retained a trace of the last soul who went to tell it divine things of sentiment.

The paintings of cherubs, made with a great brush, were faded; and in the heraldic green vault echoed the supplications, their mysticism long dead, of those who had come to pray to God.

The alabaster of the baptismal font had lost its immaculate whiteness, and the missal was left in a state of waiting on the lectern.

Leaning over the bell towers, a stately calm perished of boredom.

I went up to the organ, and when I played a chord, a strange noise came from inside it.

Frightened, I wanted to flee when a group of bats fell at my feet, terrified; others, setting off in circular flight, disappeared into the roof.

XXIX

I draw back the curtain of the past and remember . . .

She's sick; she has a fever and is delirious.

Her burning little hand, resting on mine, has the sweet confidence of a bird in its nest.

Her little body in pain suffers, just as a leaf trembles in the wind.

She doesn't want anything. Her blue eyes, like two miracles of the sky, gaze into the distance, oblivious of the outside world; perhaps they are in a bed of sapphires, the place where they were born.

I've scattered all my tenderness over her little bed, covering it with the warmth of my sobbing.

Now she looks at me, and her gaze of a dream has the heavenly clarity of emotion.

These powerful eyes lift my soul from the depths of its bitterness to the surface of life; the life I do not want, the life I scorn.

"Here I am," they tell me, "live for me."

I did not listen to that sublime appeal, and forever lost those eyes which had made my soul more gentle, in the same way the bandage cushions the sting of the wound.

Life passes, my incomplete life of a puppet begging for love; and she, the divine creature snatched from my arms by the savage claw of fate, does not know my pain.

She also suffers without knowing it, because the sorrow of my great love casts an invisible frozen shadow over her heart.

Two words, the most enormous that language has invented, might unite us; but no one will pronounce them, as indifference has silenced peoples' hearts. She and I, separated by the world and united by a sublime love of the soul, will die, waiting for mercy.

XXX

Like faces covered in veils, stars pass behind the clouds; and the waning moon bathes in the river.

A strange harmony of voices gives life to the scenery. The singing of toads and crickets and the plaintive howling of dogs come together, and in a single thrust go to die in the silvery reaches.

Ferryboats cross the canals with the mild sway of the seagull, sinking the wings of their oars in the shifting ribbon of gray water.

The violin's notes drift like petals of a lily along the river, setting off on an unknown course. From very far away, airy pilgrims arrive in white flocks to tell each other their adventures of love, taking shelter under the loose tresses of desolate willows.

Anuarí has come to lie on his back at the bottom of my little gondola, and his gaze is paralyzing; he drives a needle between my eyebrows and presses it into my brain.

Thrilled by art and idealism, I surrender my soul to the spirit of my dreams, to my marvelous Anuarí.

XXXI

Hats give me the impression of cut-off, mummified heads, and the ones with colorful dangling cords make me imagine heads pulled off by a brutal hand, still attached by a bloody vein.

I can never see a pair of gloves without imagining them to be the skin of preserved hands; and in those of a yellow color, I see something revolting that is beginning to rot.

How I loathe the items of clothing left on the bed, forgotten; there's a great parallel between them and the dead.

Once, in an asylum, I saw a mad woman who was dead, and she looked just like a violet rag tossed into a coffin.

XXXII

The giant of twilight leans toward the earth with the absorption of the faithful before the figure of Christ.

His pupils, intense, searching, flash over the sands edging the river, and rest their somber gaze on treetops and roofs of houses.

The city softens its sounds; everything moves toward rest. The downcast men, silent, drag themselves like shadows, carrying the agonizing weight of the dying titan on their heads.

Lying back on the balcony, I drink the first light of the stars, and think of the infinite sadness that a loveless heart will feel, and the heartbreaking inquietude of a heart that lives to love! . . .

Does love really exist, or is it only a longing to reflect oneself in another being, so as to better love oneself?

Love is the first embryonic force that ruptures the chaotic solitude of the spirit; it indicates the path, the energy and the vigor of living.

But does love exist?

What, then, is this strange deluge which overwhelms my being, bringing me such evil, and such good?

Anuarí, tell me: what sensation does my soul experience when your eyes contemplate it with their gentle expression?

What is it that unfurls in me like wings, to meet what radiates from you?

Where has my substance gone? Why does it all dissolve before my eyes, which grow wider in their yearning to fix you in memory, in the same way an arrow is embedded in an ancient tree trunk?

Anuarí. Is this love, by chance?

If so, then the stars must love each other a lot; the stars, which send each another the twinkling of their lights, just as your eyes and mine do when they meet.

XXXIII

Anuarí, I have not seen your spiritual beauty today, and I'm thirsty for it.

You are the most pure spring of love and art, where I satisfy my thirst for idealisms.

When you permeate me with your light, I feel springtime in me with all its music of sighs and blossoming of flowers.

Anuarí, when you leave me, I'll only have the energy to dig into the earth, eager to meet my grave.

If it were possible to fall asleep in the thrumming of life's wingbeat, like a dream . . .

If the soul could release itself from corporeal bonds, living in the air like atoms, and only return to the world at moments of happiness . . .

Will death be to dream, or will death be a dream frozen in terror?

Is it true that we do not have souls, and that there is only one single enormous soul in the Universe, everything for the one who can feel and mute for the one unaware?

Yes, Anuarí; that soul, when we look for it, comes and gives itself up to us, drowning us on its profound waterwheel of mysteries and tremendous sensations.

This soul has brought you to me, as a very rich present moment, in the arms of love.

Anuarí, why haven't you given me the warmth of your gaze; why do you leave me alone in the bloody clutches of ennui?

XXXIV

My hair falls out, and the first sadness of nightfall darkens the circles under my eyes.

The misfortunes of life have marked my face with their fatal stamp.

My mouth, which laughed in happiness, is no longer mine; today it pretends to laugh and its miserable grimace seems an omen of horror.

I have nothing; nothing . . . !

Poor shipwrecked debris, poor once-shiny rag of silk, poor light that flickers like the dying.

As old dancers drag the remains of magnificent stage dresses through their houses, so do I drag along my life, insolent in its ridiculous pomp of ironic laughter, feverish joys, poisoned triumphs.

And I live, because it is cowardice to die; and I hide my sobbing because the century doesn't understand this hysterical sentimentality.

And so they say the legend of the Clown only exists in the imagination.

When I hear this, I laugh as a dead person might laugh from the depths of the earth: a dead person whom they claim is alive.

XXXV

The flower-eating faun, in love with the white chastities of the forest and enchanted with living, runs here and there, leaping amidst the crags of the brook, pretending to laugh at the trees, looking sidelong at the sun.

His mischievous billygoat hooves scrape the earth, and tread the undergrowth, while his restless hands pull out flowers along the way.

More than anything else, the faun prefers rose petals, which he steals from the sleeping nymphs.

After he takes them, he disappears in fright, believing himself to be chased by legions of angry gods; and on the road his wild little hooves mark out a joyful rhythm, harmonizing with the sounds of the forest.

The faun has a sweet tooth, and hidden amidst the grasses he keeps an eye on the sun's work of ripening the fruits.

When he sees a ripe fruit, rose-colored like an afterglow, he approaches it with caution, tucking his little horned head into his shoulders, stretching out his shy hand and looking all about him to avoid surprises; then he plucks the fruit and goes off to eat it in the thick of the forest. With sensuality he sinks his feline teeth into the velvet flesh, delighting to see the fruit's juice run down his arms like diluted silk.

The mischievous faun is a terror for the young nymphs, and the only hope for those already grown-up.

XXXVI

The moon breaks its pale harmony on the pillars of the long corridor.

The shadow of my body runs next to me, bearing my restlessness.

Both of us seek the shelter of a pair of arms; and in the immense solitude, sick with love, both of us gaze into the night, waiting for the beloved.

White roses are draped on the gates, as on a wedding mattress; the lilies of the meadow offer me an immaculate bed.

In the atmosphere there is an erotic inquietude, and in the entire garden, a warm desire for possession.

Nostalgic birds cry out from the absence of their dead loves, while the crystal-clear fountain surrenders its song of passion to the wind.

I shout, and the echo of my voice frightens me; it's an echo that comes from the depths of myself, a tortured spasmodic echo; the painful echo of a being who has never managed to satisfy the thirst for love that consumes her.

I've screamed just as the beast howls at the mountains, in an explosion of sentimentality that it doesn't understand.

Anuarí, where are you?

Don't you hear the fervent prayer my soul addresses to you, on the verge of its own abyss?

You, who are the genie of good, why don't you soften my pain?

The lilies are expecting us, their shiny little heads nestled into one other, and the night awaits your arrival before it spreads the sparkling tulle of its immense canopy.

Anuarí, nature elevates the magisterial hymn of love into the infinite.

XXXVII

Nothingness. Tired of running about the reaches above and penetrating into the underground passages of the world, in an eagerness to forget myself, I end up in my own heart.

To forget oneself as the madman forgets his current life, dedicating his mind to what is gone.

How to uproot the sorrow of the soul? How to erase the past?

Where to find sweetness, if its source has dried up for me?

Where to find happiness, if I'm prohibited from passing through the doors of its garden?

Where to find calm, if death doesn't remember me?

If my arms could stretch further than my agony, crossing over mountains, they'd reach happiness.

Nothingness! . . . The efforts of my mind to lift themselves to the upper reaches are useless. To strangle the voice of the heart achieves nothing!

XXXVIII

I long to feel myself beneath the sun, like a little thing that doesn't suffer the pain of thinking, and gives out a gentle fragrance.

I wish I could scatter myself in the plants and flowers, like colors, like a scent; and die in the buds, mingled with the particles of pollen, to give food to the bees that come to sip nectar.

I wish I could fold my wings, like a nocturnal bat, and stay asleep until I forget that I have a soul.

I wish . . . So much do I wish, that I have nothing . . .

XXXIX

I walked without a destination, sunk in the monotony of the afternoon, without hearing any sound but my own steps.

Alone I went, down who knows what street, in who knows what country.

All at once a violet light illuminated the nostalgic gray of my thoughts; I looked, and a door of the church offered me the pale smile of its sentimental *vitreaux*.

Tragic memories passed through my mind, and feeling myself shudder with bitterness, I penetrated into this enclosure of the faithful.

A secret fear made me bend my knees before the figure of a Christ that seemed to smile at me with mercy. I was there for a long time, a very long time, living in the past and resurrecting all that lay buried as dead within my soul.

I remembered the peace of a monastery which became a holy refuge in a period of unspeakable sorrow.

What deep grief my heart revealed to the bosom of an angelic mother who murmured to me as if I were a child!

Cecilia she was called, and her tone was so tender when she talked to me, like she was uttering prayers.

And I was alone, I had nobody but her.

I was alone, my heart plunged into the cold of the grave, my head collapsed in pain, my arms stretched out. I was looking for a soul; a soul who felt sympathy for me.

If only it were possible to express in words the anguish, the loathsome black desolation of my sorrow.

Everything passed as the gale passes, razing the fields, but a very tender memory of gratitude remained within my heart for that woman dedicated to the service of Christ, who became a mother to me of the most sublime mercy.

For a long time I was at the feet of that pale Christ; beneath the caress of the sentimental *vitreaux*.

I remembered! . . .

Isn't life an eternal remembering of sadnesses?

XL

I seek a pair of lips as a source of oblivion; I seek a pair of eyes to draw back the blue veils of the reaches above and show me life's true cause.

I seek a pair of arms to embrace me, laying a garland of unknown flowers around my neck: flowers that give off warm perfumes and anesthetize.

I seek you, Anuarí!

For me there's no greater beauty than what you bring to me.

The air you stir as you walk, I desire so that I may breathe something of you.

Wherever you absorb the light, within that light I wish to dwell, even if I'd have to become a drop of water or an invisible atom.

Anuarí, in your eyes alone you incarnate everything that I've ever dreamed, everything that I would have been able to love.

In the heart of the night, I'll give myself to you with the bliss of an artist surrendering to her work, and with the grateful enthusiasm she'd feel upon surrendering to whoever created her.

No one will interrupt our divine nuptials; we will celebrate them in absence from life, when nothing shows us that we exist in others, when possessing each other entirely I come into being with you: spirit and God.

Anuarí, at that moment all of the celestial bodies will kiss, and the whitest flowers will lose their petals.

XLI

I hear the laughter of children. I hear little silken steps run along the carpet . . .

Everything is illusion; I don't find happiness anywhere.

The depth, the depths! Suffocate, spirit in the depths! My heart! Learn to live; do not grow disturbed!

My heart! How tremendous is the price of your glory! You ask for Being itself.

Only in pain can I satisfy my thirst for the infinite. Pain! You torture me, but without you I could not live; my thought would freeze, like petrified stone.

I hear the sobbing of a child.

Everything is illusion . . .

XLII

If the planet were to fall silent and stop whirling through the reaches above, the strength of my pain would make it revive, as a dead lake would revive if a river flowed into it.

XLIII

The evil fairy of the waters has come to amuse herself on the surface of the water. She's a mad bacchante made of opalescent Chinese flames, and she dances on the waves like light.

Her very long hair unfurls itself in metallic strands and flutters in the wind, breaking into a thousand fantastic colors.

With her deep eyes of uncut emerald, the fairy hypnotizes the horizons, diminishes them, crushes them.

She dances and dances, without tire; her loud laughter takes refuge in the rocks, producing more harmony than the sound of waves.

Her tunic, which covers her frozen limbs and silvery scales, floats on the waters like the gentle sway of debris after shipwreck.

As the tide rises, drawn by the moon, the maddened fairy accelerates her dance, and the contortions of her body become spasmodic convulsions that look indistinct in the sky, like blurred lights.

A meteor passes, lashing the firmament with its radiant tail; frightened, the fairy plunges into the depths of the ocean.

In the place where her very long hair disappears, an octopus emerges, gripping the sickness of my spirit in its tentacles; a strange sickness, a very strange sickness of love.

XLIV

Anuarí! Magical spirit of my life!

Anuarí, with a flourish of generosity, you've given me unknown sweetnesses, for which I will thank you on bended knee.

Anuarí, why are you so cruel? Don't you see my agony?

I kept watch in mirrors for your arrival, and glimpsed your figure in the blurry beams of the lamp. You didn't come, and my agitation ended in a faint that made me fall headfirst into bed, and hug myself moaning against the pillows.

Anuarí, don't you see how I find my lost happiness in your eyes?

Do you know I've scorned all men to give myself only to you, most pure spirit?

Anuarí, it terrifies me to think that someday you'll no longer come, and I'll be left stretching out my arms blindly, waiting for you in a rending of the soul, now without end . . .

Anuarí, Anuarí!

Stay within me.

I'll be more faithful than your shadow, and better to you than the mother who brought you into the world.

XLV

Portrait; let me kneel before you and recite my prayer of memory and love.

Let my tenderness ascend straight into the sky, like the perfumed cloud of an incense burner.

Portrait, dissolve your gaze in me, like a fresh waterfall in a desolate meadow.

Take on life, portrait, and stretch your arms to me so I can throw myself into them.

Speak to me, portrait, with the musical voice of a bugle, and whisper into my ear entrancing words of sentiment.

Portrait, by the magic of love transform yourself into a being for a moment, and come lay yourself down on my heart.

There is no greater truth than in lies.

XLVI

Grieg has come back to life under the caress of a few tapering fingers.

The piano has set free a flock of frightened birds from its case, which have gone to shatter themselves against the windowpanes.

The carpet's been covered in sickly flowers, scattered by a dying hand with very blue veins; and someone, whom I sense and don't see, slowly says goodbye to life.

All the souls who lived in love have vanished now into mirrors, and in the dusk a woman prays, crying.

Her tears break away, one by one, falling into a crystal goblet.

The Angelus bell rings, spreading good intentions throughout the world, and the specter of the celestial abyss is delirious with ecstasy.

XLVII

Unfathomable, somber mysteries of pale twilights, which resurrect in the soul what has been and create nostalgia for what has never existed.

Hour when the beauty of sorrow deepens, an hour that fascinates like the eyes of a magician.

Twilight is the miracle of day, a prologue of things that are hinted at and float in vagueness through the world's imagination.

I adore the violet tones and iridescent lights of the afternoon because they bathe the earth in languidness, sick with intensity.

A tortured heart gets along well with the sad whims of the sun, in its death throes.

XLVIII

Furtive shadows, entering through closed blinds, have decorated my ceiling with the whim of an artist.

It's a pygmy city with only a fragile spider for inhabitant, legs like pins.

The smoke from little sticks of sandalwood, burning in a corner, imitates the shape of a slender dancer, lengthening its blue until it's cut off like an elastic band.

A Chinese mask dies of laughter, hanging against the wardrobe.

The portraits whisper in terror at such motiveless hilarity, taking care not to be heard by the hat splayed on the sofa, like a just cut-off head.

The dresser drawers yawn, showing the whiteness of shirts and stuck-out pink tongues of ribbons, as the knob of the bedpost carries out bronze argument with a pair of shoes which indignantly protest the drunkenness of their heels.

A glove makes strange faces against the wall; it suffers from the same spasms as those dying on mortuary sheets.

The city of my ceiling has grown dark, and the trembling spider has gone to hide away in its threads, which hang like a hammock from one corner to another.

All the heroes of novels roaming in confusion through shadow have returned to my shelves, looking for the pages of their books, as souls in purgatory return to the cemetery on the appointed day.

In the head of Nothingness, an idea has killed itself.

XLIX

World. If my eyes were not worn out from crying, they'd spill tears to make you feel something, until they formed a spring for you to quench your inexhaustible thirst for cruelty.

World, if I could make you understand all my bitterness, I wouldn't hesitate to split my heart open and throw it at your feet.

But I already know that Mercy is a phrase, just as I know that for you Pain is a lie.

A PARTIAL LIST OF SNUGGLY BOOKS

G. ALBERT AURIER *Elsewhere and Other Stories*
S. HENRY BERTHOUD *Misanthropic Tales*
LÉON BLOY *The Desperate Man*
LÉON BLOY *The Tarantulas' Parlor and Other Unkind Tales*
ÉLÉMIR BOURGES *The Twilight of the Gods*
JAMES CHAMPAGNE *Harlem Smoke*
FÉLICIEN CHAMPSAUR *The Latin Orgy*
BRENDAN CONNELL *Jottings from a Far Away Place*
BRENDAN CONNELL *Unofficial History of Pi Wei*
RAFAELA CONTRERAS *The Turquoise Ring and Other Stories*
ADOLFO COUVE *When I Think of My Missing Head*
QUENTIN S. CRISP *Aiaigasa*
QUENTIN S. CRISP *Graves*
LADY DILKE *The Outcast Spirit and Other Stories*
CATHERINE DOUSTEYSSIER-KHOZE
   The Beauty of the Death Cap
BERIT ELLINGSEN *Now We Can See the Moon*
BERIT ELLINGSEN *Vessel and Solsvart*
ENRIQUE GÓMEZ CARRILLO *Sentimental Stories*
EDMOND AND JULES DE GONCOURT *Manette Salomon*
REMY DE GOURMONT *From a Faraway Land*
GUIDO GOZZANO *Alcina and Other Stories*
EDWARD HERON-ALLEN *The Complete Shorter Fiction*
RHYS HUGHES *Cloud Farming in Wales*
J.-K. HUYSMANS *Knapsacks*
COLIN INSOLE *Valerie and Other Stories*
JUSTIN ISIS *Pleasant Tales II*
JUSTIN ISIS (editor) *Marked to Die: A Tribute to Mark Samuels*
JUSTIN ISIS AND DANIEL CORRICK (editors)
   Drowning in Beauty: The Neo-Decadent Anthology

VICTOR JOLY *The Unknown Collaborator and Other Legendary Tales*
MARIE KRYSINSKA *The Path of Amour*
BERNARD LAZARE *The Gate of Ivory*
BERNARD LAZARE *The Mirror of Legends*
BERNARD LAZARE *The Torch-Bearers*
MAURICE LEVEL *The Shadow*
JEAN LORRAIN *Errant Vice*
JEAN LORRAIN *Fards and Poisons*
JEAN LORRAIN *Masks in the Tapestry*
JEAN LORRAIN *Monsieur de Bougrelon and Other Stories*
JEAN LORRAIN *Nightmares of an Ether-Drinker*
ARTHUR MACHEN *N*
ARTHUR MACHEN *Ornaments in Jade*
CAMILLE MAUCLAIR *The Frail Soul and Other Stories*
CATULLE MENDÈS *Bluebirds*
CATULLE MENDÈS *For Reading in the Bath*
CATULLE MENDÈS *Mephistophela*
ÉPHRAÏM MIKHAËL *Halyartes and Other Poems in Prose*
LUIS DE MIRANDA *Who Killed the Poet?*
OCTAVE MIRBEAU *The Death of Balzac*
CHARLES MORICE *Babels, Balloons and Innocent Eyes*
DAMIAN MURPHY *Daughters of Apostasy*
DAMIAN MURPHY *The Star of Gnosia*
KRISTINE ONG MUSLIM *Butterfly Dream*
PHILOTHÉE O'NEDDY *The Enchanted Ring*
YARROW PAISLEY *Mendicant City*
URSULA PFLUG *Down From*
ADOLPHE RETTÉ *Misty Thule*
JEAN RICHEPIN *The Bull-Man and the Grasshopper*
DAVID RIX *A Blast of Hunters*
FREDERICK ROLFE (Baron Corvo) *Amico di Sandro*

FREDERICK ROLFE (Baron Corvo)
An Ossuary of the North Lagoon and Other Stories
JASON ROLFE *An Archive of Human Nonsense*
BRIAN STABLEFORD (editor)
Decadence and Symbolism: A Showcase Anthology
BRIAN STABLEFORD (editor) *The Snuggly Satyricon*
BRIAN STABLEFORD *The Insubstantial Pageant*
BRIAN STABLEFORD *Spirits of the Vasty Deep*
BRIAN STABLEFORD *The Truths of Darkness*
COUNT ERIC STENBOCK *Love, Sleep & Dreams*
COUNT ERIC STENBOCK *Myrtle, Rue & Cypress*
COUNT ERIC STENBOCK *The Shadow of Death*
COUNT ERIC STENBOCK *Studies of Death*
MONTAGUE SUMMERS *The Bride of Christ and Other Fictions*
GILBERT-AUGUSTIN THIERRY *The Blonde Tress and The Mask*
GILBERT-AUGUSTIN THIERRY *Reincarnation and Redemption*
DOUGLAS THOMPSON *The Fallen West*
TOADHOUSE *Gone Fishing with Samy Rosenstock*
TOADHOUSE *Living and Dying in a Mind Field*
RUGGERO VASARI *Raun*
JANE DE LA VAUDÈRE *The Demi-Sexes and The Androgynes*
JANE DE LA VAUDÈRE
The Double Star and Other Occult Fantasies
JANE DE LA VAUDÈRE *The Priestesses of Mylitta*
JANE DE LA VAUDÈRE *Syta's Harem and Pharaoh's Lover*
AUGUSTE VILLIERS DE L'ISLE-ADAM *Isis*
RENÉE VIVIEN AND HÉLÈNE DE ZUYLEN DE NYEVELT
Faustina and Other Stories
RENÉE VIVIEN *Lilith's Legacy*
RENÉE VIVIEN *A Woman Appeared to Me*
TERESA WILMS MONTT *In the Stillness of Marble*
KAREL VAN DE WOESTIJNE *The Dying Peasant*

www.ingramcontent.com/pod-product-compliance
Lightning Source LLC
Chambersburg PA
CBHW060500080526
44584CB00015B/1503